THE BIG EASY CUTE CATS

LARGE PRINT COLORING BOOK

H.R. Wallace Publishing

ISBN-10: 1-5091-0262-0
ISBN-13: 978-1-5091-0262-4

www.ingramcontent.com/pod-product-compliance
Lightning Source LLC
LaVergne TN
LVHW081254100826
845148LV00009B/1219